WHAT'S INTUITION?

Adam Bellamy

Enslow Publishing
101 W. 23rd Street
Suite 240
New York, NY 10011
USA

enslow.com

Published in 2018 by Enslow Publishing, LLC.
101 W. 23rd Street, Suite 240, New York, NY 10011

Library of Congress Cataloging-in-Publication Data

Names: Bellamy, Adam, author.
Title: What's intuition? / Adam Bellamy.
Description: New York, NY : Enslow Publishing, 2018. | Series: All about my senses | Includes bibliographical references and index. | Audience: Grades K-3
Identifiers: LCCN 2017002290| ISBN 9780766087224 (library-bound) | ISBN 9780766088016 (pbk.) | ISBN 9780766088023 (6-pack)
Subjects: LCSH: Intuition--Juvenile literature.
Classification: LCC BF315.5 .B445 2018 | DDC 153.4/4--dc23
LC record available at https://lccn.loc.gov/2017002290

Printed in the United States of America

Photo Credits: Cover, p. 1 Patrick Foto/Moment Open/Getty Images; pp. 3 (left), 10 JPagetRFPhotos/Shutterstock.com; pp. 3 (center), 6 szefei/Shutterstock.com; pp. 3 (right), 12 Kenishirotie/Shutterstock.com; p. 4 Studio Grand Ouest/Shutterstock.com; p. 8 JGI/Jamie Grill/Blend Images/Getty Images; p. 14 Morsa Images/DigitalVision/Getty Images; p. 16 Sharon Pruitt/EyeEm/Getty Images; p. 18 Flying Colours Ltd/Photodisc/Getty Images; p. 20 leungchopan/Shutterstock.com; p. 22 Andy Dean Photography/Shutterstock.com; cover, p. 1 background adapted from Flavio Edreira/EyeEm/Getty Images.

Contents

Words to Know

dangerous

friend

hunch

Intuition is a feeling I cannot explain. There is no reason for it.

Sometimes, I know that my friend is sad. I don't know why for sure, but I have a pretty good guess. This is intuition.

Sometimes, when I meet someone new, I know we will become good friends. This is intuition.

Sometimes, I know that I shouldn't do something because it could be dangerous. This is intuition.

Sometimes, intuition is called a "hunch," or "following my gut."

I have known what someone was going to say before they said it. This is intuition.

I have felt sad after I saw someone else was sad. This is intuition.

Intuition tells me to stay away from someone who is not safe for me to be around. I don't really have a reason. I just feel it.

I have guessed my birthday present. This is my intuition.

My intuition helps keep me safe and happy.

Read More

Isadora, Rachel. *I Hear a Pickle: and Smell, See, Touch, & Taste it Too!* New York, NY: Nancy Paulsen Books, 2016.

Macnair, Patricia. *Sensational Senses!* London, England: Egmont, 2016.

Reade, Clara. *Intuition: The Sixth Sense.* New York, NY: PowerKids Press, 2014.

Websites

ABCYa.com
www.abcya.com/five_senses.htm
Fun cartoons help you learn about your senses.

Science for Kids
www.scienceforkidsclub.com/senses.html
Learn more about the senses.

Index

Guided Reading Level: D
Guided Reading Leveling System is based on the guidelines recommended by Fountas and Pinnell.

Word Count: 154

APR   2018